INSIDE THE
NFL

ARIZONA
CARDINALS

BY TODD RYAN

SportsZone

An Imprint of Abdo Publishing
abdobooks.com

abdobooks.com

Published by Abdo Publishing, a division of ABDO, PO Box 398166, Minneapolis, Minnesota 55439. Copyright © 2020 by ABDO Consulting Group, Inc. International copyrights reserved in all countries. No part of this book may be reproduced in any form without written permission from the publisher. SportsZone™ is a trademark and logo of Abdo Publishing.

Printed in the United States of America, North Mankato, Minnesota
022019
092019

THIS BOOK CONTAINS
RECYCLED MATERIALS

Cover Photo: Ric Tapia/AP Images
Interior Photos: Mark J. Terrill/AP Images, 5, 8; David J. Phillip/AP Images, 7; Pro Football Hall of Fame/AP Images, 11; Harry L. Hall/AP Images, 12; AP Images, 15, 23, 43; NFL Photos/AP Images, 19; Bob Schutz/AP Images, 21; George Gojkovich/Getty Images Sport/Getty Images, 25; Chad Surmick/AP Images, 27; John Cordes/Icon Sportswire/AP Images, 31; Tom Hauck/AP Images, 33; Matt York/AP Images, 35; Gene J. Puskar/AP Images, 37; Ross D. Franklin/AP Images, 38

Editor: Patrick Donnelly
Series Designer: Craig Hinton

Library of Congress Control Number: 2018965782

Publisher's Cataloging-in-Publication Data

Names: Ryan, Todd, author.
Title: Arizona Cardinals / by Todd Ryan.
Description: Minneapolis, Minnesota : Abdo Publishing, 2020 | Series: Inside the NFL | Includes online resources and index.
Identifiers: ISBN 9781532118364 (lib. bdg.) | ISBN 9781532172540 (ebook)
Subjects: LCSH: Arizona Cardinals (Football team)--Juvenile literature. | National Football League--Juvenile literature. | Football teams--Juvenile literature. | American football--Juvenile literature.
Classification: DDC 796.33264--dc23

TABLE OF
CONTENTS

CHAPTER 1

SUPER BOWL!
FINALLY!

The last time the Cardinals had played for a National Football League (NFL) title was 1948, when they played in Chicago, and a new invention called television was all the rage.

When the 2008 regular season concluded, it did not seem as if the Arizona Cardinals should be eagerly preparing to celebrate a championship. Sure, they qualified for the playoffs. But just barely. Arizona was blown out twice in the final three weeks of the regular season. This included a 47–7 loss to the New England Patriots.

The Cardinals slunk into the postseason with a 9–7 record. Their defense was not exactly scaring off opponents. In addition, they would have to win three games to qualify for their first Super Bowl. Their chances seemed slim.

The Cardinals' Larry Fitzgerald makes a leaping catch against the Philadelphia Eagles in January 2009.

Then a strange thing happened. The defense began to perform better than it had all year. The Cardinals held down the Atlanta Falcons' explosive offense in the first round of the playoffs. They stuffed the Falcons' running game and intercepted two passes in a 30–24 home victory. They followed it up with their best defensive game of the season. Arizona recorded five interceptions in a surprisingly lopsided 33–13 win over the host Carolina Panthers.

Now anything seemed possible. The Cardinals hosted the National Football Conference (NFC) Championship Game against the Philadelphia Eagles. They had a chance to make their Super Bowl dream come true. But that wonderful dream appeared to be turning into a nightmare when the Eagles scored three second-half touchdowns to take a 25–24 lead.

That is when veteran Cardinals quarterback Kurt Warner was at his best. He drove his team 72 yards

NUMBERS CAN LIE

It's not surprising that few fans and sports media members believed that the 2008 Cardinals could reach the Super Bowl with their defense. After all, they gave up an average of 26.6 points per game during the regular season. They surrendered 56 points in one game against the New York Jets, 48 points in another against Philadelphia, and 47 in yet another against New England. The Cardinals collectively outscored their opponents by just one point (427–426) in 16 games before the playoffs. But they got hot just in time.

✗ Kurt Warner threw 30 touchdown passes and was named to the Pro Bowl in 2008.

down the field and threw a touchdown pass to running back Tim Hightower with 2:59 to play. Then the Arizona defense held on to clinch a 32–25 victory. The dream was reality. The Cardinals were in the Super Bowl.

"I always dreamed it, and it's finally here," said Adrian Wilson, the Cardinals' Pro Bowl safety. "The Arizona Cardinals

✕ Fitzgerald breaks away for a 64-yard touchdown reception in Super Bowl XLIII.

changed their stripes today. Nobody gave us a chance. Nobody gave this organization a chance."

Few thought the Cardinals would defeat the tough Pittsburgh Steelers in the Super Bowl, either. But Warner and the wide receiver trio of Larry Fitzgerald, Anquan Boldin, and Steve Breaston helped the Cardinals take a 23–20 lead late in the game. Fitzgerald scored two touchdowns, including a go-ahead 64-yard reception with 2:37 left.

The Steelers and Cardinals were headed for one of the most thrilling finishes in Super Bowl history—and it came

HIGH-FLYING WIDEOUTS

The 2008 Cardinals became only the fifth team in NFL history to feature three players with 1,000 receiving yards in one season. Wide receivers Larry Fitzgerald (1,431 yards), Anquan Boldin (1,038 yards), and Steve Breaston (1,006 yards) all exceeded that milestone.

In the ensuing postseason, Fitzgerald had the finest playoff run ever for a wide receiver. In four games, including the Super Bowl, he caught 30 passes for 546 yards and seven touchdowns. All three numbers set NFL postseason records.

Fitzgerald took the league by storm after joining the Cardinals in 2004. He was named to the Pro Bowl every year from 2007 to 2013 and in 11 of his first 14 years in the NFL.

down to the final minute. But when Steelers quarterback Ben Roethlisberger fired a 6-yard touchdown pass to wide receiver Santonio Holmes with 35 seconds remaining, Arizona was finished. The Cardinals may have lost 27–23, but they were not losers.

"I am so proud to be a part of this football team," Warner said after the game. "I think that is one of the reasons why [the defeat] doesn't hurt as bad as it could. These guys have exceeded expectations."

Of course, rock-bottom expectations for the Cardinals had been established decades before the team arrived in Arizona.

CHAPTER 2

EARLY SUCCESSES, EARLY FAILURES

Those who think the Cardinals are fairly new because they arrived in Arizona in 1988 will have to think again.

When the Cardinals franchise was born, the president of the United States was William McKinley, television had yet to be invented, and the country was involved in the Spanish-American War.

It was in 1898 when a neighborhood team representing the Morgan Athletic Club began competing in Chicago. The team was called the Normals, because it played its home games at Normal Park on Chicago's South Side. In 1901 the team began to wear uniforms that owner Chris O'Brien referred to as "cardinal red." He then changed the team's name to the Cardinals.

Cardinals Hall of Fame running back Ernie Nevers poses for a photo in 1930.

✗ Cardinals owner Charles W. Bidwill, *left*, running back Charley Trippi, and coach Jimmy Conzelman chat after Trippi signed his record-setting contract in January 1947.

The team disbanded in 1906 because there were simply not enough opponents to compete with. But the Cardinals returned in 1913. They captured the Chicago Football League title in 1917. In 1920 they joined the new American Professional Football Association (APFA), which became the NFL two years later.

The Cardinals quickly established themselves as one of the premier teams in the NFL. They finished with non-losing records in each of their first six seasons. They won the league championship in 1925 by compiling an 11–2–1 record.

Since there were no playoffs until 1933, that regular-season mark was good enough to earn them the NFL title.

Chicago doctor David Jones bought the team in 1929 and signed fullback Ernie Nevers, its first star player. Nevers made an immediate impact on Thanksgiving Day that same year. He scored an NFL-record 40 points with six touchdowns and four extra points in a 40–6 win over the archrival Chicago Bears. The game had been billed as a showdown between Nevers and Bears star Red Grange.

A MAN OF DEDICATION

The Chicago Cardinals were among the NFL's worst teams in the 1930s and 40s. The squad was overshadowed in its own town by the more successful Chicago Bears. Further competition arose in 1946 when the All-America Football Conference was formed and put a team called the Rockets in that city.

Team owner Charles W. Bidwill, who bought the Cardinals in 1933, was tired of losing money on the team. He loved football and he wanted to win. So in 1947 Bidwill outbid the Rockets for the services of University of Georgia running back Charley Trippi, who signed a contract worth $100,000, an unheard-of amount at that time.

The Cardinals were finally ready to win. But Bidwill died in April 1947, just after he had compiled a championship-caliber squad. His wife, Violet, assumed control of the team for the next 15 years.

The Cardinals were fortunate to land Nevers after his standout college career at Stanford University. He was also a fine baseball and basketball player who signed professional contracts in those sports, too. Nevers began his pro football career with the Duluth Eskimos in 1926. They actually changed their name to the "Ernie Nevers Eskimos" in his honor. He played three years with the Cardinals, from 1929 to 1931, and was an All-Pro selection in each of those seasons.

Jones sold the team to Charles W. Bidwill in 1932. This started the current period of Bidwill family ownership. But the purchase did not begin an era of prosperity. The Cardinals enjoyed a winning season in 1935 and then collapsed. They compiled a record of 12–70–3 from 1938 to 1945. In the last three of those seasons, they were a miserable 1–29. They failed to win any games in 1943 or 1944.

One reason for those failures was that the Cardinals lost more players to military service during World War II (1939–1945) than most of the other NFL teams. Among those players were quarterback Johnny Clement, wide receiver Billy Dewell, and lineman Joe Kuharich.

For two decades, Chicago Cardinals fans could only see their favorite team win an NFL championship in their dreams.

✕ *From left*, the Cardinals' Million Dollar Backfield of Elmer Angsman, Paul Christman, Pat Harder, and Charley Trippi take to the air in 1948.

But in 1947, the "Dream Backfield" turned their dreams into reality.

The Dream Backfield also was known as the "Million Dollar Backfield." It consisted of quarterback Paul Christman and running backs Pat Harder, Elmer Angsman, and Charley Trippi. The quartet performed brilliantly that season for coach and future Pro Football Hall of Fame inductee Jimmy Conzelman.

Fueled by the Dream Backfield and a strong defense, the Cardinals raced out to a 7–1 start. They finished 9–3 and clinched a title game showdown in Chicago against the Philadelphia Eagles.

The heroes of the regular season proved to be the heroes of the championship game. Angsman sprinted for two 70-yard touchdowns. Trippi added a 44-yard scoring run and 75-yard punt return for a touchdown. Angsman finished with 159 rushing yards.

Meanwhile, the defense made three interceptions and held future Hall of Fame running back Steve Van Buren to 1.4 yards per carry. And when Cardinals defensive back Marshall Goldberg intercepted a pass from Eagles quarterback Tommy Thompson in the fourth quarter, a 28–21 victory and the title were assured.

The Cardinals gave their fans more than their fair share of thrills in 1948. They won the Western Division title and compiled an 11–1

TWO TRAGEDIES IN TWO YEARS

In October 1947, Cardinals rookie punter Jeff Burkett was killed in a plane crash in Utah. He was leading the NFL in punting average at the time. The tragedy forced Charley Trippi to take over the punting duties. He later said that he thought about Burkett every time he dropped back to punt. The next year, Cardinals tackle Stan Mauldin died of a heart attack in the locker room after the first game of the 1948 season.

regular-season record. But the Eagles gained revenge in an NFL Championship Game rematch by shutting them out 7–0 in a raging blizzard in Philadelphia.

Conzelman retired that year, and the Cardinals embarked on another long losing spell. They managed just one winning season throughout the 1950s and had a 33–84–3 record during that time.

At that point, owner Violet Bidwill decided she'd had enough. She was tired of losing. She was tired of the Cardinals playing second fiddle in Chicago to the far more popular Bears. And the NFL wanted a team in St. Louis, Missouri, which appeared to be a promising market. So the league gave Bidwill permission to move her team to St. Louis.

SLIP-SLIDING AWAY

The Cardinals' last season in Chicago, in 1959, was not a memorable one. They finished the season 2–10 and lost their final six games. They even played two of their home games in Minneapolis. It is no wonder the team moved to St. Louis. From 1945 to 1959, the Cardinals averaged about 25,000 fans per game in Chicago. They hit rock bottom in 1951, averaging just 17,500 fans per game at home. It was not until the mid-1960s that attendance in St. Louis showed a considerable improvement.

CHAPTER 3

NEVER QUITE GOOD ENOUGH

The Cardinals could not escape the basement of the NFL standings merely by fleeing for St. Louis. What they needed was more talented players. Starting in 1960, they began to find them.

That was the year running back John David Crow blossomed into a star. He broke the team single-season record by rushing for 1,071 yards. The Cardinals also drafted running back Larry Wilson, then converted him into a safety. Wilson quickly developed into one of the finest players in the NFL. And that same year, wide receiver Sonny Randle caught 62 passes, including a league-best 15 for touchdowns.

The Cardinals were no champions. But they were much improved from their Chicago days. It seemed all they needed

Offensive lineman Dan Dierdorf was a standout for the Cardinals in the 1970s.

was a consistent and talented quarterback. And in 1963, they discovered that they already had one on their roster. His name was Charley Johnson.

In his first full year as the team's starting quarterback, Johnson led the Cardinals to a 9–5 record, their best since 1948. He set four team records that season, including most passing yards (3,280) and touchdown passes (28). Randle and Bobby Joe Conrad combined for 124 catches, 1,981 yards, and 22 touchdowns. Tight end Jackie Smith, linebacker Larry Stallings, and cornerback Pat Fischer also provided fresh talent.

But the Cardinals grew tired of sharing rickety old Sportsman's Park with the baseball Cardinals. The team was soon offered a chance to move to Atlanta. But it remained in St. Louis with the promise of a new home field.

Busch Memorial Stadium opened in 1966 with a capacity of more than 51,000. But the team's play became inconsistent.

WONDERFUL WILSON

Who is the best defensive player in Cardinals history? It could very well be safety Larry Wilson. Wilson recorded 52 interceptions for the Cardinals from 1960 to 1972 and led the NFL with 10 in 1966. He earned eight Pro Bowl selections from 1962 to 1970.

✕ Cardinals tight end Jackie Smith, a member of the Pro Football Hall of Fame, played for St. Louis from 1963 to 1977.

Johnson and Fischer, who had 10 interceptions, led the Cardinals to a 9–3–2 record in 1964. After that year the Cardinals could not sustain a positive trend. Each winning season in 1964, 1966, 1968, and 1970 was followed by a losing season. When the defense was strong, the offense was not. And when the offense excelled, the defense struggled.

Finally in 1974, the Cardinals put it all together. They won their first seven games on the way to winning the NFC East title, clinching their first playoff berth since 1948. Second-year coach Don Coryell drove the players to have a winning attitude.

"We take nothing for granted now," Smith said after the Cardinals started out 4–0. "My first few years here, we'd look at a couple of games as easy, so that we would have a tendency to ease up and slack off. Now it's just impossible to approach a game that way. That's what gives me the best feeling about our potential. That complacent attitude will never be part of this team."

A new generation of Cardinals led the way in 1974. The young stars included quarterback Jim Hart, wide receiver Mel Gray, running backs Terry Metcalf and Jim Otis, defensive back Roger Wehrli, and Pro Bowl offensive linemen Dan Dierdorf and Conrad Dobler.

WHAT A STEAL!

In 1962 the Cardinals obtained place-kicker Jim Bakken. He had been drafted in the seventh round that same year by the Los Angeles Rams. Little did anyone know that Bakken would blossom into one of the premier kickers in the NFL. He booted the ball for the Cardinals for 17 seasons and led the NFL in field goals made in 1964 and 1967. By the time he hung up his cleats, he had kicked 282 field goals and scored 1,380 points.

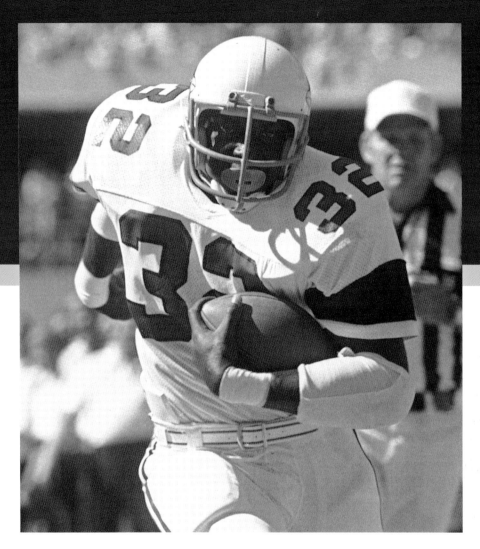

X Ottis Anderson, shown in his rookie year of 1979, rushed for 1,000 yards in five of his first six seasons for the Cardinals.

However, the Cardinals stumbled in the first round of the 1974 playoffs, losing to the Minnesota Vikings 30–14. They maintained their momentum by winning 11 of 14 games and a second straight division title the next year. But they were dominated again in the playoffs in a 35–23 loss to the Los Angeles Rams.

Two years later, Coryell left to coach the San Diego Chargers. The Cardinals never really recovered in St. Louis. For the third time in their history, they suffered through a long losing stretch. They managed just three winning seasons from 1977 to 1987 and never got close to the playoffs.

In 1978 the Cardinals created a buzz by hiring Bud Wilkinson as their coach. Wilkinson had never coached in the NFL. But he

DON CORYELL

Until Ken Whisenhunt transformed the Cardinals into NFC champions during the 2008 season, Don Coryell was the most successful coach in team history. Coryell also was among the greatest innovators in NFL history.

Coryell joined the Cardinals after coaching college football at San Diego State. He brought an exciting offensive style to the NFL with an emphasis on passing. But it was not until he began coaching the San Diego Chargers in 1978 that he began an era of explosive aerial attacks in the NFL. Among Coryell's strategies was to use the tight end heavily in the passing offense. Behind his "Air Coryell" attack, the Chargers quickly became one of the most feared offensive teams in the NFL. But his defense was never strong enough to lead to a championship.

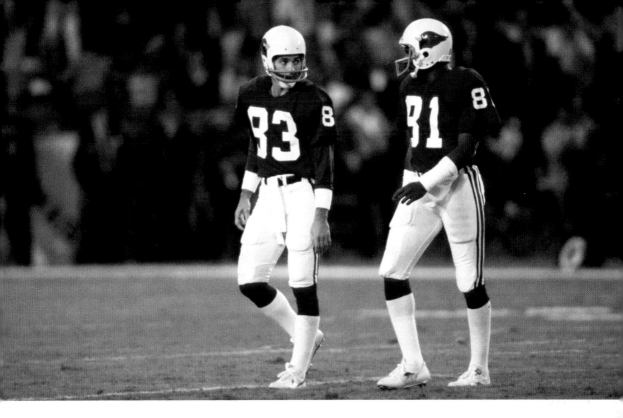

Pat Tilley (83) and Roy Green were two of the Cardinals' top receivers in the 1980s.

had been a highly successful coach at the University of Oklahoma. His two seasons in St. Louis, however, were regrettable. He coached the team to a 9–20 record before stepping down.

The Cardinals did manage a couple good years in the 1980s. In fact, they crept over .500 every season from 1982 to 1984 with one of the best offenses in the NFL. Leading the way were running back Ottis Anderson, quarterback Neil Lomax, and wide receiver Roy Green.

Soon, though, the Cardinals were moving to the desert.

CHAPTER 4

RELOCATING
TO ARIZONA

By the late 1980s, Cardinals owner Bill Bidwill, son of Charles and Violet, had become disappointed. Attendance at home games in St. Louis was low. It fell to a meager average of about 28,000 per game in 1987.

Bidwill had been pushing for new stadium to attract more fans. But he was unable to convince local officials to help pay for it. So he moved the team to Arizona. There the team would be known as the Phoenix Cardinals and play in spacious Sun Devil Stadium on the campus of Arizona State University.

St. Louis fans did not show the same outrage that those in other cities, such as Baltimore and later Cleveland, expressed when their NFL teams skipped town. When the Cardinals left,

Stump Mitchell was one of the Cardinals' offensive stars who made the move to Phoenix.

the St. Louis Post-Dispatch newspaper polled fans as to whether they were angrier about the football team's move or about the departure of slugger Jack Clark from the St. Louis baseball team. The results ended up in a virtual tie.

The Cardinals did not fare much better in Arizona—at least for quite a while. The weather was hot. But the team was not. The Cardinals continued to lose. Their defense remained one of the worst in the NFL for several years. And when the defense showed signs of improvement, the offense collapsed. The team officially changed its name to the Arizona Cardinals before the 1994 season. The idea was to show an appreciation for fans from other areas of the state.

Those fans were briefly excited when the team won four of its final five games in 1993 and then hired colorful Buddy Ryan as coach. Attendance jumped significantly in 1994 as the Cardinals won half their games. But they went 4–12 a year later and Ryan lost his job.

Replacement Vince Tobin finally guided the Cardinals to their first winning season in Arizona and a playoff spot in 1998. The team overcame a below-average defense thanks to young quarterback Jake Plummer, who passed for 3,737 yards, mostly to wide receivers Frank Sanders and Rob Moore. Those two combined for 2,127 receiving yards. Meanwhile, All-Pro cornerback Aeneas Williams shut down the opponents' best receivers.

The Cardinals were given little chance to win their first-round showdown at Dallas. After all, the Cowboys had beaten them twice in the regular season, including a 38–10 thrashing in Week 1. But needing a victory to advance, the Cardinals won 20–7, their first playoff victory since the 1947 NFL Championship Game.

The excitement soon ended when the Cardinals lost to the Minnesota Vikings in the second round of the playoffs. Those who believed the success of 1998 was a sign of things to come were quickly disappointed. The Cardinals slid back into the doldrums, going 41–87 without a winning season from 1999 to 2006.

AENEAS WILLIAMS

Aeneas Williams wasn't considered a great player coming out of high school. He was a walk-on at tiny Southern University in Louisiana. But he eventually led the nation in interceptions as a senior. He was selected by the Cardinals in the third round of the 1991 NFL Draft. Williams started his career on the right foot when he was named the 1991 NFC Defensive Rookie of the Year after posting six interceptions in his first season in the pros. He played 10 years with the Cardinals and four years with the St. Louis Rams. Williams was named to the Pro Bowl eight times and inducted into the Pro Football Hall of Fame in 2014.

AN AMERICAN SOLDIER

In 2002 Cardinals safety Pat Tillman walked away from the NFL and enlisted in the US Army. He said he felt compelled to do something after the country was attacked by terrorists on September 11, 2001. Tillman joined the elite Army Rangers and began serving in Afghanistan.

Tillman was a great football player before he left to serve his country. He was the Pac-10 Conference Defensive Player of the Year in 1997 at Arizona State University. He was drafted by the Cardinals in 1998 and set a team record for tackles in one season for Arizona in 2000.

Tillman's story ended tragically. He was killed in April 2004 by accidental fire from one of his fellow rangers. He received multiple awards from the military for his service. The Cardinals and Arizona State honored Tillman by retiring his jersey number 40. Tillman was inducted into the College Football Hall of Fame in 2010.

In 2000, voters in Maricopa County approved an initiative that helped fund the construction of a new stadium for the Cardinals. The team began play at University of Phoenix Stadium in Glendale, a suburb of Phoenix, in 2006. The stadium also hosted the Super Bowl after the 2007 and 2014 seasons.

The Cardinals drafted wide receivers Anquan Boldin and Larry Fitzgerald in 2003 and 2004, respectively. One year later the team signed Super Bowl–winning quarterback Kurt Warner

✗ Cardinals safety Pat Tillman enlisted in the US Army in 2002 and died in 2004 while serving in Afghanistan.

as a free agent. Together, the group developed into one of the league's most dangerous passing attacks.

The Cardinals improved to 8–8 in 2007. Warner threw for 27 touchdowns that year. Fitzgerald had 100 catches for 1,409 yards and 10 touchdowns. Boldin added 71 receptions for 853 yards and nine touchdowns.

Then came the thrill of the 2008 season. Arizona's passing attack was even stronger. Warner threw for 4,853 yards and 30 touchdowns. Fitzgerald, Boldin, and fellow wide receiver Steve Breaston each had 1,000 receiving yards. The Cardinals' defense struggled in the regular season but played well enough in the playoffs to help the team make the surprise run to the Super Bowl. The Cardinals lost 27–23 to the Pittsburgh Steelers in Super Bowl XLIII. But Arizona was understandably excited about its prospects for 2009.

The Cardinals continued to feature an exciting passing attack led by Warner, Fitzgerald, and Boldin that season. Arizona went 10–6 and won its second straight NFC West title.

The Cardinals played host to the Green Bay Packers in a truly wild wild-card game. Arizona pulled out a 51–45 victory in overtime in the highest-scoring game in NFL playoff history. Warner was nearly flawless, completing 29 of 33 pass attempts for 379 yards and five touchdowns.

SOUTH OF THE BORDER

The Cardinals and San Francisco 49ers made history as the first NFL teams to play a regular-season game outside the United States. The contest was held in Mexico City's Estadio Azteca on October 2, 2005, before 103,467 fans. It was the largest crowd to witness an NFL regular-season game. And to make matters sweeter for the Cardinals, they won 31–14.

✗ Kurt Warner throws a pass in November 2008. Warner played his final five seasons with Arizona and led the team to a Super Bowl before he retired in January 2010.

The Cardinals won when linebacker Karlos Dansby returned a fumble 17 yards for a touchdown.

The Cardinals were overwhelmed the next week in a 45–14 road loss to the New Orleans Saints. The Saints went on to win the Super Bowl, while the Cardinals marked another key turning point in franchise history.

CHAPTER 5

SEARCHING FOR SUCCESS

Kurt Warner announced his retirement from the NFL on January 29, 2010, at the age of 38. He had played 12 seasons in the league. Warner went undrafted after completing his college career at the University of Northern Iowa. He stocked shelves at a grocery store in Iowa before the St. Louis Rams gave him a shot in 1998. His career then took off.

"It's been an amazing ride," Warner said at the press conference announcing his retirement. "I don't think I could have dreamt it would have played out like it has, but I've been humbled every day."

Warner's departure cast doubt on the team's future. But he had shown that the long-suffering Cardinals could soar to great heights.

Kurt Warner announces his retirement in a press conference at the Cardinals' training facility in Tempe, Arizona.

Arizona finished 5–11 in its first season without Warner. Derek Anderson took over at quarterback. He was one of three Cardinals to start at least three games at quarterback that season as the Cardinals struggled to find Warner's successor.

In 2012, head coach Whisenhunt and the Cardinals started 4–0, and the team looked to be back to its winning ways. However, Arizona went on to lose nine consecutive games. This led to Whisenhunt being fired on December 31, 2012.

New head coach Bruce Arians had proved himself as the offensive coordinator for the Indianapolis Colts. He also served as the team's interim head coach when Chuck Pagano was diagnosed with cancer.

Arians came in and found success early with Arizona. The Cardinals went 10–6 in his first season in 2013 but just missed the playoffs. In 2014 he coached the team to an 11–5 record. It was one of the best regular seasons in franchise history, but the Cardinals finished second in the NFC West and had to settle for a wild-card spot. That meant they had to open the playoffs on the road at Carolina. To make matters worse, the Cardinals were without starting quarterback Carson Palmer and backup Drew Stanton, who were injured. Behind inexperienced

x Carson Palmer had one of the best seasons of his career with the Cardinals in 2015.

third-stringer Ryan Lindley, the Cardinals came up short against the Panthers, 27–16.

Like Warner, Palmer had come in as a veteran and revitalized his career in Arizona. The former Cincinnati Bengals

✗ Larry Fitzgerald bulls his way into the end zone for the game-winning touchdown against the Packers in the 2015 NFL Playoffs.

star had his best season with Arizona in 2015. Palmer thrived with the Cardinals, connecting with Larry Fitzgerald and fellow receiver John Brown for more than 2,200 yards worth of passes during the season. Arizona rode the NFL's No. 1 offense to a

13–3 record, the NFC West title, and the team's first-ever first-round bye in the playoffs.

The Cardinals hosted the Packers in a NFC divisional-round thriller. It looked like Arizona had it wrapped up until Packers quarterback Aaron Rodgers completed a 41-yard Hail Mary touchdown pass on the final play of regulation to tie the game 20–20. But on the first play in overtime, Fitzgerald caught a short pass from Palmer and took it 75 yards to the Packers' 5-yard line. The two hooked up again two plays later for the game-winning touchdown. That sent Arizona back to the NFC Championship Game for the first time since 2009.

DAVID JOHNSON

Arizona had established veterans on offense in 2015 with Carson Palmer and Larry Fitzgerald. The Cardinals' youth came in running back David Johnson, their third-round draft pick that spring. Johnson was key to Arizona reaching the NFC Championship Game as he scored 13 touchdowns as a rookie. He was even better in his second season, when he scored 20 touchdowns and ran for more than 1,200 yards. He was out most of 2017 with injuries but had already shown the potential to be a star in Arizona for years to come.

The Cardinals headed back to Carolina for a rematch with the Panthers, this time feeling confident with a healthy Palmer under center. Unfortunately for the Cardinals, the outcome was no different. Palmer threw four interceptions and lost two fumbles as the Panthers won it going away, 49–15.

The 2015 season proved to be the peak for Arizona and Palmer. The Cardinals finished the next two seasons a combined 15–16–1. This led to Arians and Palmer each retiring after the 2017 season. Arians was the winningest coach in team history when he announced his retirement.

Big changes were in store for Arizona heading into 2018. The Cardinals used their first-round draft pick to select Josh Rosen out of the University of California, Los Angeles (UCLA), hoping he'd become the team's franchise quarterback. It was the first time the team had used its No. 1 pick on a quarterback since 2006, when the Cardinals drafted Southern Cal's Matt Leinart.

They also selected Steve Wilks as their next head coach. He came over from Carolina, where he had been the defensive coordinator for one year and coached the Panthers' defensive backs for five seasons before that. But 2018 was a nightmare. Running back David Johnson returned from injury but was mostly ineffective as he tried to regain his form. Rosen threw only 11 touchdown passes and was intercepted 14 times. And the defense was the worst in the NFL against the run as the Cardinals slumped to a 3–13 finish.

Wilks was fired at the end of the season and replaced by former Texas Tech head coach Kliff Kingsbury. A former quarterback himself, Kingsbury coached 2018 NFL MVP Patrick Mahomes at Texas Tech. The Cardinals hoped he could guide Rosen to similar success in the years to come.

It certainly helped that Johnson showed signs of his old form late in 2018. Also, in January 2019, Fitzgerald announced that he would be back for a sixteenth season with the Cardinals. That gave Rosen two important weapons as he tried to establish himself in the NFL and get the Cardinals back on track. It had been more than a decade since Arizona's magical Super Bowl run. Cardinals fans were hungry for a return to the spotlight.

PATRICK PETERSON

Arizona made the most of its first-round draft pick in 2011 when it selected cornerback Patrick Peterson. He instantly became a steady contributor on defense and special teams. Peterson did not miss a game in his first eight seasons while recording 23 interceptions and establishing his reputation as a shutdown corner. Peterson also made a name for himself as a punt returner. In his rookie year, he returned four punts for touchdowns. Peterson was voted to the Pro Bowl in each of his first eight seasons in the NFL.

TIMELINE

A football team later known as the Cardinals begins playing in Chicago.

The team is purchased by painting and decorating contractor Chris O'Brien and adopts its current nickname.

The Cardinals win the Chicago Football League title.

The franchise joins the APFA, which becomes the NFL in 1922.

The Cardinals clinch the NFL title on December 12 by virtue of their 11–2–1 record.

1898

1901

1917

1920

1925

The team is bought by Charles W. Bidwill. The move marks the beginning of family ownership that still stood as of 2018.

The Cardinals earn their only win in an NFL Championship Game with a 28–21 victory over the Philadelphia Eagles in Chicago on December 28.

The team plays in its second consecutive league title game but falls 7–0 to the Philadelphia Eagles on December 19.

Citing a lack of fan support, owner Violet Bidwill moves the franchise to St. Louis.

The Cardinals earn their first playoff spot since 1948 with a 10–4 record. But they lose 30–14 in the first round to the Minnesota Vikings on December 21.

1932

1947

1948

1960

1974

The Cardinals lose the lead in the final minute of the Super Bowl and fall to the Pittsburgh Steelers 27–23 on February 1.

After going 9–7 in the 1998 season the Cardinals win their first playoff game since 1947, beating the Dallas Cowboys 20–7 on January 2.

The Cardinals hire Ken Whisenhunt as head coach.

Owner Bill Bidwill moves the franchise to Arizona.

Coach Don Coryell guides the Cardinals to their second consecutive postseason berth.

2009

2007

1999

1988

1975

The Cardinals slip to 3–13 and first-year head coach Steve Wilks is fired. He is replaced by Kliff Kingsbury.

Bruce Arians retires as the winningest head coach in franchise history.

The Cardinals reach the NFC Championship Game before losing to the Carolina Panthers.

Bruce Arians leads the Cardinals to the playoffs in his second year as head coach.

Whisenhunt loses his job after the Cardinals finish 5–11 for the second time in three years.

2018

2017

2015

2014

2012

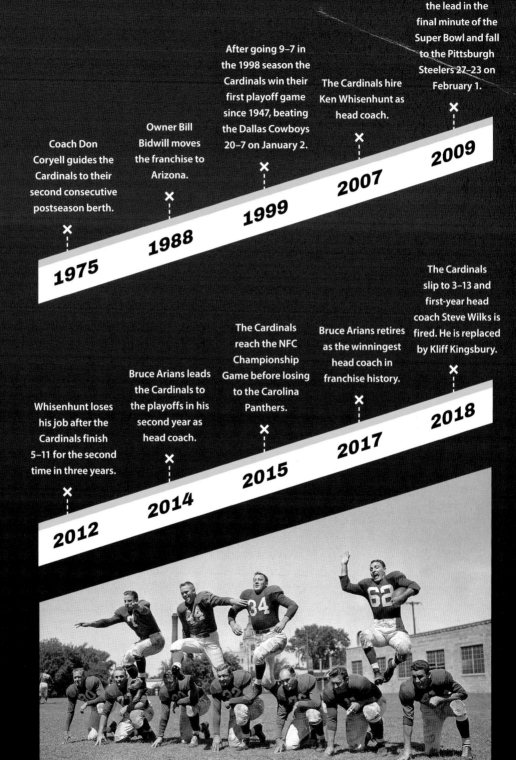

43

QUICK STATS

FRANCHISE HISTORY

Racine Cardinals (1920–21)
Chicago Cardinals (1922–59)
St. Louis Cardinals (1960–87)
Phoenix Cardinals (1988–93)
Arizona Cardinals (1994–)

SUPER BOWLS

2008 (XLIII)

NFL CHAMPIONSHIP GAMES *(1933–69, wins in bold)*

1947, 1948

DIVISION CHAMPIONSHIPS *(since 1970 AFL-NFL merger)*

1974, 1975, 2008, 2009, 2015

KEY COACHES

Bruce Arians (2013–17): 49–30–1,
 1–2 (playoffs)
Jimmy Conzelman (1940–42,
 1946–48): 34–31–3, 1–1
 (playoffs)
Ken Whisenhunt (2007–12): 45–51,
 4–2 (playoffs)

KEY PLAYERS *(position, seasons with team)*

Ottis Anderson (RB, 1979–86)
Dan Dierdorf (OT, 1971–83)
Darnell Dockett (DT, 2004–13)
Larry Fitzgerald (WR, 2004–)
Jim Hart (QB, 1966–83)
Dick "Night Train" Lane
 (CB, 1954–59)
Ollie Matson (RB, 1952, 1954–58)
Ernie Nevers (FB, 1929–31)
Patrick Peterson (CB, 2011–)
Luis Sharpe (T, 1982–94)
Jackie Smith (TE, 1963–77)
Charley Trippi (RB–QB, 1947–55)
Kurt Warner (QB, 2005–09)
Roger Wehrli (CB, 1969–82)
Aeneas Williams (CB, 1991–2000)
Larry Wilson (S, 1960–72)

HOME FIELDS

State Farm Stadium (2006–)
 Previously known as University
 of Phoenix Stadium
Sun Devil Stadium (1988–2005)
Busch Stadium (1966–87)
Sportsman's Park (1960–65)
Soldier Field (1959)
Comiskey Park (1922–25, 1929–58)
Normal Field (1920–21, 1926–28)

*All statistics through 2018 season

QUOTES AND ANECDOTES

The Chicago Cardinals lost so many players to military service during World War II that they were forced to merge with the Pittsburgh Steelers to form one club in 1944. Without much time to come together as a team, they lost all 10 games that season.

For a short time in the early and mid-1960s, the NFL paired up the teams that finished second in their respective divisions for a game known as the "Playoff Bowl." The Cardinals defeated the Green Bay Packers 24–17 in the Playoff Bowl on January 3, 1965.

Dan Dierdorf, an NFL Hall of Famer who was perhaps the greatest offensive lineman in Cardinals history, went on to a sterling career as a color commentator on NFL television broadcasts. He served for many years on the *Monday Night Football* crew in the 1980s and 1990s.

Most running backs run the ball far more often than they catch it. Such was not the case with Cardinals back Larry Centers, who was a pass-catching specialist. Centers racked up an amazing 101 receptions for 962 yards in 1995. In the process, he became the first NFL running back to catch more than 100 passes in a season.

One of the things that made former Cardinals coach Bruce Arians famous was the type of hat he wore. Most coaches wear a baseball-style cap. Arians, however, wore a flat hat that looked like something an old-fashioned golfer might wear. Arians was proud of his style and created his own fashion line of hats. The proceeds went to benefit his charitable foundation.

GLOSSARY

archrival
An opponent that brings out great emotion in a team and its players.

disband
To break up, as in a sports franchise.

elite
The highest level.

franchise
A sports organization, including the top-level team and all minor league affiliates.

Hall of Fame
A place built to honor noteworthy achievements by athletes in their respective sports.

innovator
One who has new ideas about how something can be done.

market
The city in which a team plays.

overshadow
To outshine or surpass.

Pro Bowl
The NFL's all-star game, in which the best players in the league compete.

retire
To end one's career.

rookie
A professional athlete in his or her first year of competition.

showdown
An important game.

walk-on
A college athlete who does not receive a scholarship for participating.

MORE INFORMATION

BOOKS

Gillespie, Katie. *Arizona Cardinals*. New York: AV2 by Weigl, 2016.

Wilner, Barry. *Total Football*. Minneapolis, MN: Abdo Publishing, 2017.

Ybarra, Andres. *Arizona Cardinals*. Minneapolis, MN: Abdo Publishing, 2017.

ONLINE RESOURCES

Booklinks
NONFICTION NETWORK
FREE! ONLINE NONFICTION RESOURCES

To learn more about the Arizona Cardinals, visit
abdobooklinks.com or scan this QR code. These links are
routinely monitored and updated to provide the most current
information available.

PLACE TO VISIT

Pro Football Hall of Fame
2121 George Halas Dr. NW
Canton, OH 44708
330–456–8207
profootballhof.com

This hall of fame and museum highlights the greatest players and moments
in the history of the National Football League. Among the people affiliated
with the Cardinals who have been enshrined are Dan Dierdorf, Ernie Nevers,
Kurt Warner, Aeneas Williams, and Larry Wilson.

INDEX

ABOUT THE AUTHOR

Todd Ryan is a library assistant from the Upper Peninsula of Michigan. He lives near Houghton with his two cats, Izzo and Mooch.